DEC 2003

The Lewis and Clark Expedition

CORNERSTONES OF FREEDOM™

SECOND SERIES

Christine Webster

Children's Press®
A Division of Scholastic Inc.
New York • Toronto • London • Auckland • Sydney
Mexico City • New Delhi • Hong Kong
Danbury, Connecticut

Photographs © 2003: Animals Animals/Darren Bennett: 26; Art Resource, NY: 16 (National Museum of American Art, Washington D.C.), 6, 45 center (National Portrait Gallery, Smithsonian Institution), 17 (Smithsonian American Art Museum, Washington D.C.), 12 top (Aldo Tutino/Smithsonian Institution); Corbis Images: cover bottom, 4, 18, 45 top left (Bettmann), 14 top (Lowell Georgia), 9 top (David Muench), 29 (Bob Rowan/Progressive Image); Earth Scenes: 32, 33, 44 bottom right (Michael Gadomski); FPG International/Getty Images: 7; Hulton|Archive/Getty Images: 10; Montana Historical Society, Helena: 30 bottom; National Geographic Image Collection/Richard Durrance: 25; North Wind Picture Archives: 13, 30 top (N. Carter), 3, 5, 8, 12 bottom, 15, 22, 24 top, 24 bottom, 36, 39, 44 top right; Stock Boston: 27, 45 bottom (Lionel Delevingne), 31 (John Elk III); Stock Montage, Inc.: 9 bottom (The Newberry Library), cover top, 23, 40, 41, 44 left, 45 top right; Stone/Getty Images/Tom Tietz: 14 bottom; The Image Works/Sean Sprague: 11; Viesti Collection, Inc.: 20 (Joe Viesti), 34 (Robert Winslow).

Map on page 21 by TJS Design

    Library of Congress Cataloging-in-Publication Data
Webster, Christine.
  The Lewis and Clark Expedition / by Christine Webster.
    p. cm.—(Cornerstones of freedom. Second series)
  Summary: Discusses the early nineteenth-century journey of Meriwether Lewis and William Clark through the Louisiana Purchase and beyond, for the purpose of exploring the land and establishing friendly relations with native peoples.
Includes bibliographical references and index.
  ISBN 0-516-22678-9
  1. Lewis and Clark Expedition (1804–1806)—Juvenile literature.
2. West (U.S.)—Discovery and exploration—Juvenile literature. 3. West (U.S.)—Description and travel—Juvenile literature. [1. Lewis and Clark Expedition (1804–1806) 2. West (U.S.)—Discovery and exploration.]
I. Title. II. Series.
F592.7 .W43 2003
917.804'2—dc21

                        2002009110

1 2 3 4 5 6 7 8 9 10 R 12 11 10 09 08 07 06 05 04 03

IMAGINE AMERICA WITHOUT ITS MILES of highways or crowded cities. Two hundred years ago, that is the way it was. At that time, the United States ended at the Mississippi River. Between the mighty Mississippi and the Pacific Ocean was largely unexplored land. Much of this area was part of the Louisiana Purchase, a huge expanse of territory the United States bought from France. In 1803 President Thomas Jefferson sent Meriwether Lewis and William Clark to explore a route through this territory to the Pacific Northwest. What they discovered paved the way for future explorers.

WHY THE LOUISIANA TERRITORY?

At the time Thomas Jefferson became president of the United States, two out of three Americans lived in an area within 50 miles (80 kilometers) of the Atlantic Ocean.

Thomas Jefferson was born in Virginia in 1743 inside a tiny cabin. The tall, slender, fair-skinned boy became the third president of the United States in 1801. After the Lewis and Clark expedition, Jefferson's interest in the west continued. He proceeded to send out other men to explore new areas.

In the Southwest, Spain claimed a stretch of land from Texas to California. Farther north, France claimed the area from the Mississippi River to the Rocky Mountains known as the Louisiana Territory. Much of this land was uncharted and had never been explored by whites. This territory consisted of present-day Arkansas, Missouri, Iowa, Minnesota west of the Mississippi River, North Dakota, South Dakota, Nebraska, Oklahoma, nearly all of Kansas, portions of Montana, Wyoming, and Colorado east of the Rocky Mountains, and Louisiana west of the Mississippi River, including the city of New Orleans. This area interested the United States because the land was believed to be rich in natural resources, especially furs. It was also important because it bordered the Mississippi River, a valuable **trade** route. The United States could use the port at New Orleans to trade up and down the Mississippi River with Spanish, British, and French markets that were already established and trading with Native Americans.

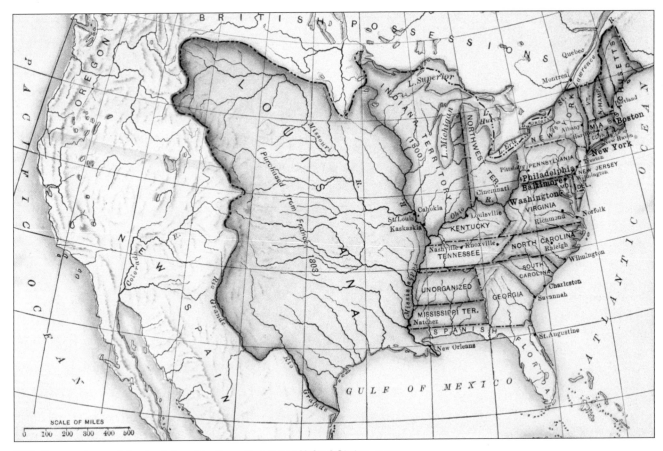

With the purchase of the Louisiana Territory, the young United States grew by almost one half.

President Jefferson made an offer to Napoleon I, the emperor of France. Jefferson wanted to purchase New Orleans for two million dollars. Instead, Napoleon agreed to sell the United States all 820,000 square miles (2,132,800 square kilometers) of the Louisiana Territory. Jefferson thought that this was a good deal. Four days before Christmas 1803, the Louisiana Territory officially became part of the United States of America. The purchase price was fifteen million dollars, about three cents per acre.

GOOD DOG

Lewis purchased a large Newfoundland dog, Seaman, for twenty dollars before the expedition. It is believed Seaman made the entire journey, although the dog is not mentioned often in the journals.

★　★　★　★

MERIWETHER LEWIS (1774–1809)

Lewis was born and raised in Virginia. He studied natural history and joined the Virginia militia, the state of Virginia's military organization, as a private soldier. (In times of emergency, the militia provided the state with military force.) After becoming a captain in the U.S. Army, Lewis became private secretary to the new president, his old friend Thomas Jefferson, in 1801.

Jefferson had begun planning an expedition to the Pacific Northwest even before completing the Louisiana Purchase. He wanted to know everything about this largely unexplored land. He appointed his young private secretary, Captain Meriwether Lewis, leader of the expedition.

At twenty-eight, Lewis was an army officer, an experienced **naturalist,** and a highly trusted aide to Jefferson. Jefferson knew Lewis had the necessary qualities to lead such a mission. The president wrote a letter to Lewis and asked for his assistance.

Jefferson wanted to learn many things from the expedition. He wanted details about the types of plants and animals found on the land, maps of the rivers and mountains, and any information about Native Americans. He hoped Lewis would learn about each tribe—their customs, their numbers, their languages. He also hoped that Lewis would be able to establish friendly relations with them. Most important,

Jefferson longed for the discovery of the Northwest Passage. This was a water route believed to link the Atlantic and Pacific oceans. If this route existed, trading would be much easier with Asia and Europe.

Lewis was well prepared to take on the tasks Jefferson wanted him to carry out. Lewis had studied with the nation's best scientists. He knew how to identify different plants, **navigate** and steer a boat, read and make maps, and even perform basic surgery. Learning surgery enabled Lewis to care for his crew and any Native Americans they met along the way. He could also pass along this knowledge to them and thereby gain the Native Americans' trust. Lewis was aware that exploring this vast and strange territory would be difficult. He would need someone to help him lead the expedition. Lewis wrote to a friend from his military days, William Clark, a man he trusted completely. Together, Meriwether Lewis and William Clark would lead an expedition that would change history forever.

WILLIAM CLARK (1770–1838)

William Clark was born in Virginia, the youngest of six brothers in a family of ten children. He and his family moved to Kentucky in 1784. Clark joined the military in 1789 and became an infantry officer. Clark was commander of a rifle company when he met Lewis.

PREPARING TO SET FORTH

Both Lewis and Clark were busy during the summer of 1803. Lewis was in Pittsburgh overseeing construction of the **keelboat** that would be used to navigate the rivers, while Clark was in Clarksville, Indiana, gathering volunteers and supplies. By mid-October Lewis had traveled down the Ohio River with a few other volunteers and joined his partner. Unfortunately, it was too late in the season to begin the expedition. They would have to wait until spring, when the ice on the Missouri River would break. They focused on building their winter quarters, Camp Wood. Finished by December, it was located 20 miles (32 km) north of St. Louis, across from the mouth of the Missouri River.

A boatload of settlers travels down the Ohio River. The Ohio was invaluable to the settlers for transportation and played an important role in the westward expansion of the United States.

This is a section of the Ohio River today in Shawnee National Forest in Illinois.

Clark and his men building their winter quarters, Camp Wood. Here, more men were recruited and trained for the upcoming expedition.

The winter provided a good opportunity for the new crew to get to know one another. The men ranged in age from eighteen to thirty-three years old. They were around forty in number, including Clark's African American **slave,** York. The crew trained, gathered supplies, and learned to follow orders.

Together, the men had all the necessary skills for such a journey. George Drouillard was a fine hunter and **interpreter;** John Colter, a woodsman; Patrick Gass, a carpenter (who later became a sergeant following the death of Charles Floyd);

RULES OF ORDER

Lewis and Clark ran a tight ship. The party followed an Orderly Book of written rules. According to their rule book, lashes were the punishment for sleeping on duty and death was the punishment for desertion (or escaping in the case of a slave). Although there were a couple of desertions, no one was executed, however.

Lewis and Clark crashing into a tree. The rivers sometimes posed hidden dangers for the expedition. This engraving is from Patrick Gass' published journal of the expedition.

William Warner, a cook; John Shields, a blacksmith; Pierre Cruzatte, a fiddler; and brothers Reuben and Joseph Field were hunters and woodsmen. Lewis and Clark assigned John Ordway, Nathaniel Pryor, and Charles Floyd the rank of sergeant. The group, made up of almost all military men, was called the **Corps** of Discovery.

They broke camp on May 14, 1804. The plan was to take their boats upstream following the Missouri River westward. They hoped to discover a westward-flowing river and then **portage** their supplies and boats over land to it. It was believed that this great river spilled into the Pacific, their final destination. If they discovered a river flowing westward to the Pacific, accessible from the eastward-flowing

Missouri, they would accomplish their goal of finding a coast-to-coast passage.

The Corps traveled in three boats. The keelboat held the major supplies of medicine, food, and gifts for Native Americans as well as their own notes. It was 55 feet (16.7 meters) long and 8 feet (2.4 m) wide and capable of carrying 10 tons (9.1 metric tons) of supplies. Two smaller boats, called **pirogues,** followed.

Proceeding up the Missouri, Lewis and Clark divided their duties according to their **expertise.** Clark stayed on the keelboat mapping and noting their course, while Lewis often walked along the shore making notes about the land, rocks, plants, and animals.

Progress was slow, and the boats often became stuck on muddy sandbars. The men of the Corps would then have to wade in the shallow waters to push the boats off. At other times the men walked along the shore pulling the boats with ropes. They traveled about 14 miles (22.5 km) per day.

The Corps used long lengths of thin, netted fabric such as this to keep out bothersome mosquitoes at night.

The days were often hot and humid with severe thunderstorms. Many men suffered **sunstroke.** They were pestered by ticks and mosquitoes. To keep away mosquitoes, they covered themselves with bear grease, which was used as an insect repellent, during the day, and netting at night. Drouillard hunted deer, beaver, and

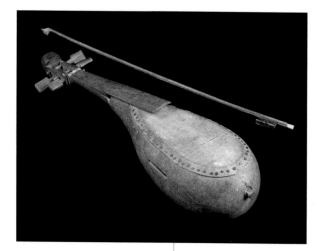

This 19th-century fiddle resembles the fiddle played by Cruzatte. After long days of traveling and exploring, music was an important form of entertainment for the men.

★ ★ ★ ★

turkeys and kept the crew well fed. The Corps spent the nights listening to Cruzatte play the fiddle or writing in their journals. By the end of August the Corps had reached the Northern border of present-day Nebraska.

ENCOUNTERING NATIVE AMERICANS

For two months, the Corps did not come in contact with any Native Americans. That changed when they entered the territory of the Otos. The Otos lived along the Missouri River, in what is now present-day Iowa, and

The Native Americans that the Corps encountered on its journey were curious about the purpose of the expedition.

were once one of the southern Sioux tribes. Many of their members had died from smallpox, so the remaining Otos were absorbed into the neighboring Missouri tribe. The Corps sent out a member, Joseph La Liberte, to locate the Otos and invite them to a council meeting. Mysteriously, La Liberte never returned, and the Corps feared he was lost or had deserted them. The following day, fourteen Otos appeared in the camp and met

The fifteen stars and fifteen stripes on this U.S. flag represent each of the fifteen states of 1804. Today the flag consists of 50 stars and thirteen stripes, representing the 50 states and the original 13 colonies.

with the Americans. The first official meeting between these representatives of the United States and Native Americans took place on August 3, 1804. A small group of Otos gathered. They wore **breechcloths,** which covered the lower part of their bodies, and painted buffalo robes.

Lewis and Clark told the Otos about the purpose of their journey and the wishes of their government. They spoke of President Jefferson as a "great father." Lewis informed the Otos that Jefferson would look out for them and promised peace if they didn't make war on whites or other tribes. Lewis and Clark even offered advice to the Native Americans on their daily lives. When they were finished speaking, they handed out specially made "peace medals," fifteen-star flags, and other gifts.

The Corps impressed the Native Americans with their compasses and air gun. The Otos were very pleased with their gifts. They promised to pursue the advice given and showed joy at having a "father" to depend on.

Scott's Bluff, in western Nebraska, would become a landmark on the Oregon Trail for pioneers making their way west across the Great Plains. Unlike many of the later pioneers, Lewis and Clark found the Great Plains to be beautiful and "well-watered."

A wild coyote prowls the long grass of the Great Plains. Coyotes became a common sight to the Corps of Discovery.

As Lewis and Clark moved farther north and west, the climate and landscape changed. The air was dry and there were few trees, but thousands of acres of thick green grass lay before them. The expedition had moved onto the Great Plains. Dozens of unfamiliar animals, such as coyotes, antelopes, and prairie dogs, came into sight. Lewis and Clark had instruments for measuring the animals, and they estimated each animal's weight. They also dried and packed away plants. Lewis and Clark preserved the plants in order to remember what kinds of plants grew in certain areas on their journey and to further study them at a later time.

They traveled through present-day South Dakota to meet with the Teton Sioux. Although the meeting with the Otos

This sketch of the leaf of an evergreen shrub appears in William Clark's journal.

had gone well, Lewis and Clark were wary of the Sioux. It was important to establish good relations with these particular Native Americans because their alliance with British traders in Canada provided them with weapons that allowed them to control the fur trade along the Missouri. The Sioux did not want the Americans to bypass them and make direct contact with other tribes.

The Corps made camp on an island near the mouth of the Bad River. The Sioux were camped 2 miles (3.2 km) up on the northwestern side. Lewis and Clark met with the Sioux and exchanged food and gifts. They gave a speech similar to the one they had given to the Otos. Nothing seemed to impress the Sioux.

FLOYD'S BLUFF

Near present-day Sioux City, Iowa, Sergeant Charles Floyd suddenly became seriously ill. He died on August 20, 1804, from what's believed to have been a ruptured appendix. The Corps buried him on a hill they called Floyd's Bluff.

Lewis and Clark decided to invite three chiefs on board their boat for some drinks. When they returned to the bank, the Sioux seized the rope of one pirogue. They said no Americans could go any farther up the river and demanded more gifts. For several minutes, tempers rose. To avoid a fight that would have jeopardized the expedition, Clark threw a five-pound bundle of tobacco twisted into the shape of a carrot at the Sioux. They released the rope. Because of the bad feelings the Corps experienced that day, Clark named the island Bad Humored Island.

FORT MANDAN

The weather turned colder as they entered the region of present-day North Dakota. Winter was coming early, and the first snow fell on October 21, 1804. The Corps of Discovery had traveled 1,600 miles (2,573 km). Their goal was to reach an area where the Mandan had villages before winter came and the river froze. Some 4,500 Native Americans lived in the five villages that belonged to the Mandan and Hidatsa nations. Two of the villages belonged to the Mandan, and the Hidatsa lived in the other three villages.

The Hidatsa people were friends and neighbors of the Mandan. The Mandan were a peaceful tribe, but the Hidatsa often sent war parties against the Shoshone nation. When the Shoshone struck back, the Mandan sometimes found themselves in the line of fire.

When the Corps reached the first of the two Mandan settlements, the tribe was pleased to see them. The Mandan

WINTER NEIGHBORS

The corps bartered with the Mandans for corn and dried vegetables when game became scarce. The blacksmith mended axes and sharpened tools and weapons. The Mandans were fascinated by the color of York's skin. They believed he had great spiritual power.

This portrait of a Mandan village was painted by George Catlin, who visited the Mandan villages where the Corps had wintered almost 30 years before. Catlin painted many of the Native American peoples that the Corps had encountered.

17

hoped that the expedition's presence would deter any Shoshone raids or attacks. The Corps and the Mandans met in a peace council, and the Corps learned that the Mandans were seldom the aggressors and only wanted peace. The council went well, and the Mandans were pleased to know the Corps planned to winter nearby.

The men searched for the perfect spot to winter and chose a wooded area across the Missouri from the lowest Mandan village. By November they had built a V-shaped structure

Sacagawea points the way to Lewis and Clark. She was invaluable to the expedition as an interpreter and guide.

* * * *

from cottonwood, with four rooms along each side and a large inner courtyard. Each room had a stone fireplace for heat and cooking. They called their winter camp Fort Mandan.

On November 4, 1804, they met a French-Canadian trader named Toussaint Charbonneau and his Shoshone wife, Sacagawea. Sacagawea had been captured from the Shoshones at a young age. Charbonneau later won her in a card game. It is believed she was fifteen years old at the time Lewis and Clark met her, and she was pregnant. Charbonneau offered his services to Lewis and Clark as an interpreter. They agreed, knowing that they would encounter the Shoshone later.

Using Sacagawea and Charbonneau as interpreters proved to be an involved process. Sacagawea spoke Shoshone and Hidatsa, and Charbonneau spoke Hidatsa and French. One of the woodsmen, Francis Labiche, spoke both French and English, while Lewis and Clark spoke only English. With this mixture of language, just trying to understand what someone said was a lengthy process. For instance, to know what a Shoshone said, Sacagawea would translate it into Hidatsa for Charbonneau. He would then translate it into French, and then Labiche would translate the French into English for Lewis and Clark. Sign language was used by all to make the translations easier.

The winter was bitter cold. One day the temperature dropped to 45 degrees below zero Fahrenheit (43 degrees below zero Celsius). Several men got frostbite, and their food supply dwindled. Christmas came and was celebrated by firing two cannons and dancing.

19

* * * *

On February 11, 1805, Sacagawea gave birth to a boy named Jean-Baptiste. He was known fondly as Pompy or Little Pomp. Lewis's journal suggests that he had nothing to do with the birth of the child, except for giving Sacagawea a medicine of crushed rattlesnake tails with water to speed her delivery.

After a long winter, the ice on the river finally melted and the river was open again. The expedition was about to set out into country, approximately 2,000 miles (3,218 km) in width, inhabited only by Native Americans.

UNCIVILIZED TERRITORY

On April 7, 1805, Lewis and Clark said good-bye to a dozen men who headed back downriver. They took the large keelboat, which was filled with maps, reports, **artifacts,** plants, and live animals back to St. Louis. Most of the material was then sent on to Washington for President Jefferson. An enthusiastic **horticulturist** and student of natural history, Jefferson eagerly awaited these discoveries. Those people remaining with Lewis and Clark were all in excellent health and happy spirits. The total party now consisted of thirty-three members, including Charbonneau, Sacagawea, and their baby.

Hundreds of buffaloes graze peacefully in North Dakota. Lewis and Clark were astounded by the size of the herds they encountered.

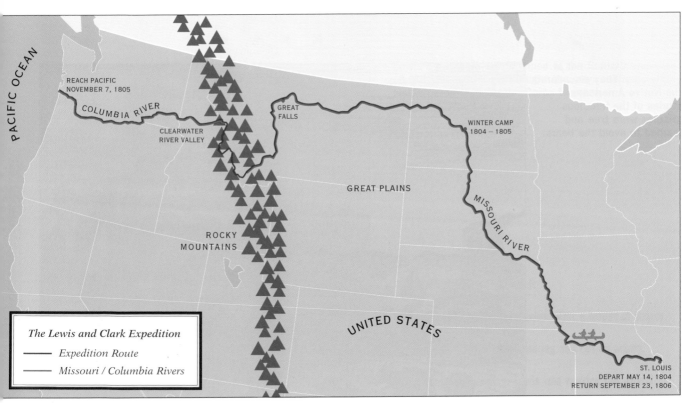

The Lewis and Clark Expedition
— Expedition Route
— Missouri / Columbia Rivers

PACIFIC OCEAN

REACH PACIFIC
NOVEMBER 7, 1805

COLUMBIA RIVER

CLEARWATER
RIVER VALLEY

GREAT
FALLS

WINTER CAMP
1804 – 1805

GREAT PLAINS

MISSOURI RIVER

ROCKY
MOUNTAINS

UNITED STATES

ST. LOUIS
DEPART MAY 14, 1804
RETURN SEPTEMBER 23, 1806

**This map traces the route
taken by Lewis and Clark
to the Pacific Ocean.**

By the end of April the Corps had passed the mouth of
the Yellowstone River in present-day North Dakota. Food
was abundant in these regions. The men saw many elk,
goats, antelope, and beaver. The Corps came across herds
of as many as 10,000 buffaloes. These giants appeared
tame and sometimes had to be pushed out of the way.
Each man ate about nine pounds of buffalo meat each day,
for breakfast, lunch, and dinner.

The Native Americans had warned Lewis and Clark
about grizzly bears. They told them that these huge bears
could withstand many arrows and survive. They said that
these bears would not be harmed by the white man's bullets.
At first, Lewis and Clark found numerous bear tracks but
did not see any bears. They thought the Native Americans

NAMED IN LOVE

On May 29, 1805, Clark discovered a clear, pretty stream, its banks adorned with roses. He named it the Judith River (right) in honor of a girl in Virginia that he hoped to (and eventually did) marry.

The flowing waters of the Marias River merge with the Missouri in northern Montana, near the present-day town of Loma.

Which river was the Missouri? Both captains believed the south fork to be the true Missouri, but the rest of the Corps disagreed. They decided to divide into two groups to study the river depths and currents. After several days of scouting, the captains were convinced the Missouri was the south fork. They felt that the other fork would lead to the plains, not the mountains. Lewis named it the Marias River after a cousin. The men were still unsure. In order to calm their doubts and uneasiness, Lewis set out on foot ahead of the others.

24

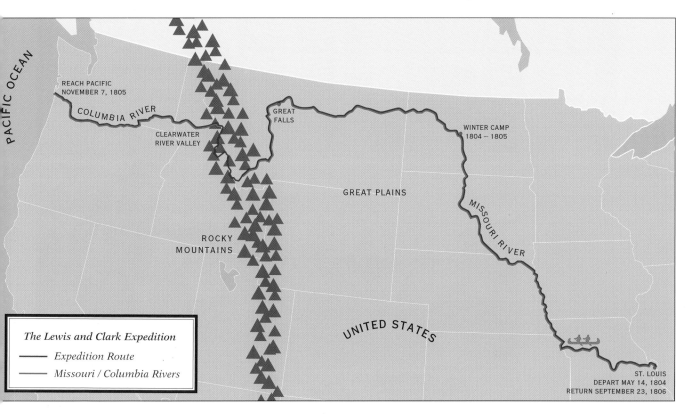

The Lewis and Clark Expedition
—— Expedition Route
—— Missouri / Columbia Rivers

PACIFIC OCEAN

REACH PACIFIC
NOVEMBER 7, 1805

COLUMBIA RIVER

CLEARWATER
RIVER VALLEY

GREAT
FALLS

WINTER CAMP
1804 – 1805

GREAT PLAINS

ROCKY
MOUNTAINS

MISSOURI RIVER

UNITED STATES

ST. LOUIS
DEPART MAY 14, 1804
RETURN SEPTEMBER 23, 1806

This map traces the route taken by Lewis and Clark to the Pacific Ocean.

By the end of April the Corps had passed the mouth of the Yellowstone River in present-day North Dakota. Food was abundant in these regions. The men saw many elk, goats, antelope, and beaver. The Corps came across herds of as many as 10,000 buffaloes. These giants appeared tame and sometimes had to be pushed out of the way. Each man ate about nine pounds of buffalo meat each day, for breakfast, lunch, and dinner.

The Native Americans had warned Lewis and Clark about grizzly bears. They told them that these huge bears could withstand many arrows and survive. They said that these bears would not be harmed by the white man's bullets. At first, Lewis and Clark found numerous bear tracks but did not see any bears. They thought the Native Americans

Lewis and Clark shoot at a grizzly bear. They discovered the Native Americans' stories of the ferocious grizzlies were true and learned to avoid the bears.

had been exaggerating, but they soon learned differently. On April 29, 1805, Lewis and another hunter killed a grizzly bear. It was the first grizzly ever to be scientifically recorded. The crew learned these creatures were not easy to kill.

On May 4, Clark and Drouillard were out hunting and shot a tremendous grizzly ten times. Even so badly wounded, the bear roared loudly and charged, swimming halfway across the river to a sandbar, where it took twenty minutes to die. The bear measured 8.5 feet (2.6 m) tall with over 4-inch (10-centimeter) claws. After that, Lewis's dog, Seaman, was on constant alert for any further bear encounters.

Lewis caught his first glimpse of the Rocky Mountains on May 26, 1805. He thought the snowcapped peaks would be difficult for the Corps to cross.

SEAMAN AND THE BEAVER

On May 19, 1805, Seaman swam after a wounded beaver. The beaver bit him in the hind leg and cut an artery, causing severe bleeding. Lewis was worried the wound would be fatal, but Seaman recovered.

A short while later, Lewis, for the first time, saw what he thought was the Rocky Mountains. For a moment he stood in awe but he quickly realized that tough times lay ahead. The Rockies looked impassable. Within 100 miles (161 km) of the mountains, the expedition hit a snag. On June 2, 1805, they reached a **fork** in the Missouri that the Hidatsa had not warned them about.

★ ★ ★ ★

NAMED IN LOVE

On May 29, 1805, Clark discovered a clear, pretty stream, its banks adorned with roses. He named it the Judith River (right) in honor of a girl in Virginia that he hoped to (and eventually did) marry.

The flowing waters of the Marias River merge with the Missouri in northern Montana, near the present-day town of Loma.

Which river was the Missouri? Both captains believed the south fork to be the true Missouri, but the rest of the Corps disagreed. They decided to divide into two groups to study the river depths and currents. After several days of scouting, the captains were convinced the Missouri was the south fork. They felt that the other fork would lead to the plains, not the mountains. Lewis named it the Marias River after a cousin. The men were still unsure. In order to calm their doubts and uneasiness, Lewis set out on foot ahead of the others.

On June 13 loud roaring sounds led Lewis to an 80-foot (24-m) drop of water crashing to foam below. Lewis had reached the Great Falls of the Missouri, which the Native Americans had told him about. Unfortunately, the pleasure was short-lived. As Lewis traveled a little farther upriver he was disappointed to discover four more waterfalls. Now the Corps would have to go out of its way by about 18 miles (29 km) in order to bypass the falls.

A DIFFICULT PORTAGE

Clark rejoined Lewis at a place they called Portage Creek. They knew that portaging around the falls was going to be a tedious journey. Portaging meant they would have to carry their boats and supplies on land around the falls to the river

Lewis called the crashing and foaming waters of Rainbow Falls "one of the most beautiful objects in nature."

A CACHE

To lighten their load, the men of the Corps made a cache, or storage place, at different places. To make a cache, a deep hole is dug. The supplies to be cached are then placed on layers of sticks and hidden within, and the earth is replaced. A cache can protect its contents for years.

A Western diamondback, a kind of rattlesnake, prepares to strike. Snake bites could be deadly, and the expedition was always on the lookout for snakes.

beyond. It was a long way to lug their supplies, particularly without horses or pack animals. Clark suggested using wagons to help carry their supplies. A large cottonwood tree was used to build two wagons, and sails were fixed on top in hope that the wind would help to push the wagons along.

* * * *

Text on sign: CONTINENTAL DIVIDE ELEVATION 7263 ft. RAINFALL DIVIDES AT THIS POINT. TO THE WEST IT DRAINS INTO THE PACIFIC OCEAN. TO THE EAST INTO THE ATLANTIC.

Today, this sign marks one spot along the Continental Divide, which extends along the Rocky Mountains from Canada to Mexico.

The Corps began the difficult journey across the rough terrain in broiling heat. Hauling their canoes and supplies was exhausting. The wheels on the wagons broke several times and had to be rebuilt with whatever could be found along the trail. High winds blew sand in their eyes, heavy rains fell, and slippery rocks cut and bruised their feet. Rattlesnakes were another hazard. Sometimes the Corps was in water all day, hauling its boats along against strong currents. On land, trouble-some prickly pears (a type of cactus with many prickles) stabbed their bodies.

It took more than a month to portage around the Great Falls. Now the Corps was weeks behind schedule. For the first time, Lewis realized the Corps would not reach the Pacific and return to Fort Mandan by winter, as he had hoped. The men, he wrote in his journal, were exhausted but cheerful. When the Corps reached the ridge of the Rockies, the captains saw that the Continental Divide would not provide them with easy portage as they hoped. In North America, the Continental Divide is a ridge of high ground that separates westward-flowing streams from eastward-flowing ones.

On July 25, 1805, the Corps reached the forks where the Missouri River splits into three smaller rivers. Sacagawea recognized the dry grassland as Beaverhead Rock, the area where her family lived. Because Sacagawea's people, the Shoshone, had horses, the Corps was eager to find their village. The expedition headed southwest up one river they named the Jefferson River, after the president. The river was shallow and swift, making it difficult to drag the canoes upstream.

On August 12, 1805, Lewis, along with Shields, Drouillard, and Hugh McNeal, came across three Shoshone women who were searching for food. The women were terrified and began to cry. Startled, Lewis lifted his shirt to show them his white skin and gave them gifts. This thrilled them. The women led them to their camp, but before they arrived, sixty warriors descended upon the Americans. Quickly, one Shoshone woman explained to the chief who they were and why they were there. This was pleasant news to the chief, and he was glad to see them. He warmly embraced Lewis.

The three men stayed with the tribe for the night to work out a trade for horses. The Shoshone were too nervous to trust the white men. Lewis invited them to the riverbank to see the goods he was offering, but the rest of the Corps was not there yet. Desperate, Lewis promised if they stayed, they would see a black man and a Shoshone woman.

* * * *

Named by Lewis after his partner in exploration, the Clark Fork River crosses the Bitterroot Mountains. This was one of the most difficult portions of the journey for the Corps.

Everything Lewis had said was proven true. Clark arrived. When the tribe saw Sacagawea with him, they were shocked. It turned out that she was the sister of their chief, Cameahwait.

THROUGH THE MOUNTAINS TO THE OCEAN

Having successfully traded for twenty-nine horses and a mule, Lewis and Clark headed out again on August 31. The expedition was accompanied by a Shoshone guide named Old Toby. Lewis and Clark asked Sacagawea to continue with them on the journey, and she agreed. They crossed the Continental Divide through what is known as the Lemhi

★ ★ ★ ★

This sign marks the route Lewis and Clark took as they traveled west up Lolo Creek.

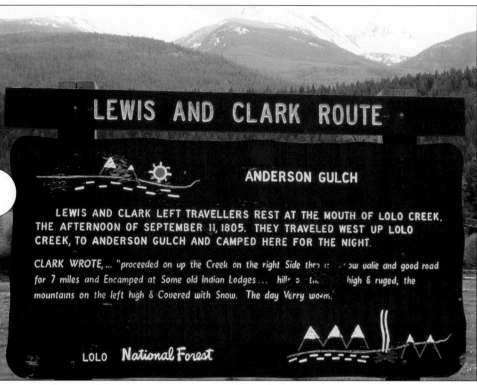

A Nez Perce hunter goes after a bison.

Pass. They crossed the Bitterroot Mountains over another pass called the Lolo Trail. Several horses slipped as they traveled up and down steep hills. Three days later, a blinding snowstorm hit, and they lost sight of the trail. There was no food; the men were exhausted, frostbitten, and sick. Clark feared they would freeze or starve to death.

Clark went ahead with six men to find food and a way out. By the time they found the trail again, many horses had died. Two days later Clark found the Nez Perce people's camp at the foot of the mountains. The Nez Perce were

* * * *

happy to feed the starving travelers, and Clark sent men back to the others with food. After eleven days in the Bitterroot Mountains, on the brink of starvation, the Corps of Discovery staggered out near present-day Weippe, Idaho, on September 22, 1805.

Lewis and Clark stayed with the Nez Perce for two weeks. They ate salmon and camas roots, the staple diet of the Nez Perce, and built new canoes. From the Nez Perce, they learned they could return to the water along a branch of the Columbia River called the Clearwater. They left their horses to be cared for by the Nez Perce until they returned. A chief named Twisted Hair agreed to guide the Corps through their country. Now traveling with the current, they traveled farther in a day than they had in a month. Sometimes the river was too fast, which caused their canoes to flip.

The cold and barren desert they now entered was rocky and windswept. The Columbian Plains are a dry and treeless

The whirling waters of the Columbia River Gorge were a challenge to the expedition, who got tossed in every direction. Fortunately, they made it through safely.

31

area, and there was little game for the expedition to hunt. The expedition then traveled from the dry desert of eastern Washington and Oregon along the Snake River to the dense rain forest of the Pacific Northwest. Finally, they reached the mighty Columbia River. The river cut through the thickly forested Cascade Mountains. The shores were a tangle of vegetation, the air was humid and hot, and it rained every day.

On November 7, 1805, the party rejoiced prematurely. They thought they had reached the Pacific Ocean, but it

The Corps of Discovery had to travel through the dense forests of the Cascade Mountains to reach the Pacific.

was only a large bay called Gray's Bay. In fact, they were still 20 miles (32 km) away from the ocean. Fierce storms and heavy winds kept them from moving on for nearly three weeks. Lewis reached the Pacific Ocean first on November 15, 1805. Clark arrived by foot three days later. They stood on a beach looking out at the Pacific Ocean, fascinated by the endless rolling waters. Lewis and Clark had reached their destination.

A GOOD GUESS

Clark estimated they had traveled 4,162 miles (6,696 km) from the mouth of the Missouri to the Pacific. He was only 40 miles (64 km) off the actual distance.

* * * *

THE FINAL WINTER

Lewis and Clark needed to decide where to spend their final winter. They held a vote on November 24, 1805, and decided to cross to the south side of the Columbia near modern-day Astoria, Oregon, to build their fort. They chose a slightly raised site in a wooded area that teemed with elk.

Visitors to the Fort Clatsop National Memorial can see what life was like for the Corps of Discovery in 1805.

⋆ ⋆ ⋆ ⋆

They cleared the land of trees and brush and built Fort Clatsop, named for a neighboring Native American tribe. The fort was large and square with rooms facing one another down each side. Lewis and Clark each had his own room. The Corps and its supplies occupied the other five rooms.

The winter was gloomy, since the days were cold and rainy. In fact, there were only twelve days that winter when it didn't rain. The Corps kept busy preparing for their trip home. They hunted, smoked the meat, made clothes from elk hides, and boiled salt water in a large kettle to make salt. The salt added flavor to their otherwise plain diet of elk meat and roots. Lewis finished listing and describing in his journals all the new plants and animals they had discovered. Clark completed the first map of the Pacific Northwest.

Everyone was anxious to return home, but it was important to wait until the right time. If they waited too long, the Missouri would freeze and the Corps would have to spend another winter on the Great Plains. If they left too early, the snow on the mountains would not have melted yet. The plan was to leave in April, but the Corps of Discovery couldn't wait until then. On March 23, 1806, the expedition headed back up the Columbia River and set off for home.

RETURNING HOME

Traveling home wasn't easy for the expedition. The Columbia was swollen with melted snow, and the current was now

A VOTE AHEAD OF ITS TIME

The captains included Sacagawea and Clark's slave, York, in the vote on where the Corps should spend its final winter. This vote was taken more than a century before women or Native Americans were granted full rights of citizenship and nearly sixty years before slaves would be freed.

35

The Blackfoot felt threatened by the Corps because if the Americans gave guns to other Native American tribes, it would weaken Blackfoot power. In an attempt to steal the Corps' guns, two Blackfoot lost their lives.

against them. The Corps had to portage around the lower Cascades in rain, and local Chinook tribes stole from them. They returned to the Nez Perce to retrieve their horses and on June 15, 1806, headed back up the Lolo Trail. Although it was spring on the Plains, it was still winter in the mountains. The snow was packed hard enough to travel on, but they couldn't see their trail. The Corps retreated down the mountains to wait for the snow to melt.

After crossing the Bitterroot Mountains again, Lewis and Clark made a crucial decision. The two captains planned to part ways. It was agreed that if they split up, they would be able to explore more of the Louisiana Territory. Clark would head south down the Yellowstone River, and Lewis would head north across a shortcut to the Great Falls and then explore the Marias River. They would meet back at the Missouri River.

When Lewis and his men arrived at the Marias, he once again divided the group in order to investigate the river's course. He took Drouillard and the Field brothers with him. On top of a **rise,** Lewis viewed the country. Alarmed, he noticed eight members of the Blackfoot tribe on horses, watching Drouillard. Although outnumbered, Lewis approached the Native Americans and explained why they were there.

Guards were put on post that night. Unfortunately, Joseph Field put his rifle down behind him while on duty. One Blackfoot crept up and took the gun, while two others stole Lewis's and Drouillard's guns. Joseph called out to his brother, who chased and caught one of the Blackfoot. Robert Field seized the gun from him and stabbed the Blackfoot.

The horses scattered, and the Blackfoot chased them. The animals climbed a bluff, and Lewis called out that he would shoot if the horses were not returned. Suddenly, one of the Native Americans jumped out from behind a rock and

NEARSIGHTED HUNTER

While out hunting, Lewis was hit by a ball in the left thigh. Lewis was certain it was a Blackfoot and yelled to retreat. He later learned it was only Cruzatte, who mistook Lewis for an elk.

another stopped ahead of him. Lewis fired quickly and shot one of them in the stomach, narrowly missing being shot himself. When the skirmish was over, two Native Americans were dead.

Heading south with most of the men and horses, Captain Clark took an easier pass and crossed the Continental Divide by July 8, 1806. He reentered the Great Plains, and downstream from the mouth of the Yellowstone River the entire expedition was reunited. The Corps of Discovery, together again, arrived back at the Mandan villages. One member, John Colter, requested permission to leave the Corps and return to the Yellowstone to trap beaver. Lewis and Clark granted him this wish. It is here that they also said good-bye to their interpreters, Sacagawea, Charbonneau, and their son, little Jean-Baptiste.

The remaining Corps raced along the Missouri current at 70 miles (113 km) per day. They paid their respects at Charles Floyd's grave. Continuing on, they soon began meeting boat after boat of American traders. Many were amazed that the Corps members were still alive.

In September of 1806 the Corps rejoiced at the sight of cows along the Missouri shore. They knew they were close to home. Finally, the journey came to an end. They arrived in St. Louis on September 23, 1806. They had been gone for nearly two-and-a-half years.

LIFE AFTER THE EXPEDITION

Meriwether Lewis and William Clark were welcomed back to the United States as national heroes. Balls, dinners, and

James Madison served as Secretary of State to Thomas Jefferson from 1801 to 1809. He later succeeded Jefferson as President of the United States in 1809.

receptions were given in their honor. In return for their sacrifices and courage in the West, Congress gave Lewis and Clark 1,600 acres (648 hectares) of land each. Every member of the corps was given double pay plus 320 acres (130 ha) of land.

Lewis became governor of the Louisiana Territory in March of 1807. By the time James Madison became president in 1809, Lewis was in serious trouble. Besides drinking too much, Governor Lewis had incurred many debts through arrangements he made between the U.S. government and gifts he traded with the Native Americans. James Madison refused to pay any of these debts. In total, Lewis faced a debt of four thousand dollars.

In 1807, Meriwether Lewis went to Philadelphia in search of a publisher for his and Clark's journals. Unfortunately, Lewis never provided the manuscripts to the publishers so he was unable to see them in print before his death. William Clark had the journals published in 1814.

Sadly, on October 11, 1809, only a little more than three years after the expedition ended, Lewis was found dead. His death was ruled suicide. In addition to his heavy drinking and being deeply in debt, Lewis suffered from severe depression. Meriwether Lewis was thirty-five years old.

When Lewis's partner, William Clark, returned home, York began asking for his freedom, which Clark refused to grant for some time. He occasionally became angry at this request. Eventually, however, Clark freed his slave, and York went on to establish a freight-hauling business in Louisville, Kentucky. Clark was appointed Superintendent of Native Affairs for the new territory and was given an important rank in the militia as a **brigadier** general. He married Julia "Judith" Hancock, for whom he had named a river, on January 5, 1808.

Always fond of Jean-Baptiste, Clark wrote to Sacagawea and Charbonneau offering to look after Jean-Baptiste and to educate him. They agreed, and in 1809 they traveled to St. Louis to leave the child with Clark. Sacagawea died on December 22, 1812, at the age of twenty-five. Eight months later, Clark officially adopted Jean-Baptiste and Sacagawea's other child, Lisette. Clark was a devoted father to all of his five children.

President James Madison appointed Clark territorial governor in 1813. The following year Clark published the journals from the expedition. He continued as governor until 1820, when the state of Missouri was created. It was this year that his beloved wife, Julia, died from an illness. Clark eventually married again. His new wife, Harriet Kennerly Radford, was a cousin of Julia's. Together they had two children. Harriet died in 1837. During his career Clark negotiated at least thirty treaties with the Native Americans. The Native Americans knew him as the Red Hair Chief. William Clark died on September 1, 1838, in St. Louis at the age of sixty-eight. He died at the home of his eldest son, Meriwether Lewis Clark.

Although Lewis and Clark didn't find the Northwest Passage, they managed to discover 172 previously unknown plants and 122 previously unknown animals. They opened doors to peaceful relations with several Native American tribes and helped introduce scientific exploration in the United States. The boundless possibilities that existed in the American West were revealed through the acts of these two courageous men.

In 1807, William Clark became a Native American agent for tribes west of the Mississippi River. His role was to organize western defenses against British and Native American attacks. He earned great respect from Native Americans.

Glossary

artifacts—anything made by humans

breechcloths—small cloths worn around the waist to discreetly cover the lower body

brigadier—an officer of rank between colonel and general

corps—a group of persons associated with each other or acting together

expertise—great knowledge or skill

fork—part of a tree or road that divides into two parts or branches

horticulturist—a person who studies the science of plants

interpreter—a person who translates for people speaking in different languages

keelboat—a shallow boat with a keel to permit sailing in the wind

naturalist—an expert in natural history

navigate—to steer or manage a boat

pirogue—a dugout boat like a canoe

portage—the act of carrying canoes, boats, and supplies
over land from one body of water to another

rise—a high point on land

slave—a person with no rights who was owned by another
person as property and could be bought and sold

sunstroke—overheating due to too much exposure to
the sun

trade—the act of buying and selling

treaty (treaties)—an agreement (or agreements)
between nations

Timeline: The Lewis

1803

JUNE 20
President Jefferson writes a letter to his secretary, Meriwether Lewis, asking him to lead an expedition across the Pacific Northwest to the Pacific Ocean.

JULY 4
The Louisiana Purchase is announced.

DECEMBER 21
The Louisiana Territory officially becomes part of the United States.

1804

MAY 14
The expedition begins up the Missouri with about forty members and Lewis's Newfoundland dog, Seaman.

JULY 4
The first July 4th celebrated west of the Mississippi. Cannons are fired and Independence Creek is named.

AUGUST 3
First official meeting takes place between the Corps of Discovery and Native Americans.

NOVEMBER 4
Lewis and Clark meet and hire Toussaint Charbonneau and Sacagawea as interpreters.

1805

APRIL 29
Lewis and another hunter kill the first grizzly bear specimen ever to be scientifically cataloged.

JUNE 13
Lewis scouts ahead and discovers the Great Falls of the Missouri.

NOVEMBER 18
Lewis and Clark reach their final destination, the Pacific Ocean.

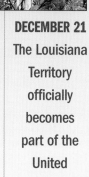

and Clark Expedition

SEPTEMBER 23
Lewis, Clark, and the rest of the Corps arrive home in St. Louis, Missouri.

OCTOBER 11
Meriwether Lewis commits suicide at an inn south of Nashville.

DECEMBER 22
Sacagawea dies. Clark assumes custody of her two children, Jean-Baptiste and Lisette.

SEPTEMBER 1
William Clark dies at the home of his eldest son, Meriwether Lewis Clark.

MARCH 23
The expedition leaves Fort Clatsop for the return journey home.

AUGUST 14
The Corps reaches the Mandan villages again. Charbonneau, Sacagawea, and Jean-Baptiste stay. One Corps member, John Colter, gets permission to return to the Yellowstone to trap beaver.

CONTINENTAL DIVIDE
ELEVATION 7,263 ft.
RAINFALL DIVIDES AT THIS POINT. TO THE WEST IT DRAINS INTO THE PACIFIC OCEAN. TO THE EAST INTO THE ATLANTIC.

To Find Out More

BOOKS AND VIDEOS

A&E. *Biography—Lewis and Clark, Explorers of the New Frontier.* Videocassette. Biography: 2000.

Bergen, Lara. *Explorers and Exploration: The Travels of Lewis and Clark.* New York: Raintree Steck-Vaughn Publishers, 2000.

Burns, Ken, dir. *Lewis and Clark—The Journey of the Corps of Discovery.* Videocassette. PBS Home Video: 1997.

Clark, William. *Off the Map: The Journals of Lewis and Clark.* New York: Walker and Company, 1998.

ORGANIZATIONS AND ONLINE SITES

Lewis and Clark National Historic Trail
700 Rayovac Drive, Suite 100
Madison, Wisconsin 53711

Lewis and Clark in the Rocky Mountains
Bitterroot National Forest
1801 N. First Street
Hamilton, Montana 59804

Lewis and Clark's Historic Trail
http://www.lewisclark.net/journals/index.html

Lewis and Clark: The Journey of the Corps of Discovery
http://www.pbs.org/lewisandclark/index.html

On the Trail with Lewis and Clark
http://www.onlineclass.com/Trail/resources.html

46

Index

Bold numbers indicate illustrations.

About the Author

Christine Webster is the author of many books for young readers. She has a special interest in United States and Canadian history. Her work for Children's Press includes titles in the series From Sea to Shining Sea and Cornerstones of Freedom. She lives in Canada with her husband and four children.